T'ai Chi

Cheng Man-ch'ing & Robert W. Smith

T'ai Chi

The "Supreme Ultimate" Exercise
for Health, Sport, and Self-Defense

TUTTLE Publishing

Tokyo | Rutland, Vermont | Singapore

Disclaimer
Please note that the publisher and author(s) of this instructional book are
NOT RESPONSIBLE in any manner whatsoever for any injury that may result
from practicing the techniques and/or following the instructions given within. Martial
arts training can be dangerous—both to you and to others—if not practiced safely.
If you're in doubt as to how to proceed or whether your practice is safe, consult with
a trained martial arts teacher before beginning. Since the physical activities described
herein may be too strenuous in nature for some readers, it is also essential that a
physician be consulted prior to training.

"All the photographs in this book are printed in reverse image to facilitate imitation of
the movements illustrated. Thus you should follow the photogaphs exactly as though
you were looking at your own reflection in the mirror. Accompanying the photographs
are diagrams showing the exact position and weighing of the feet. Note that the foot
diagrams are not reversed and hence show the position of your own feet as you stand
looking in the "mirror" of the photographs. In some cases the photographs are not
reversed and these examples are noted in the instructions."

Published by Tuttle Publishing, an imprint of Periplus Editions (HK) Ltd.

www.tuttlepublishing.com

Copyright © 1966 Cheng Man-ch'ing and Robert W. Smith
All rights reserved.

LCC Card No. 67-23009
ISBN 978-0-8048-3593-0

First U.S. edition, 1967
First paperback edition, 2004

Distributed by:

North America, Latin America & Europe
Tuttle Publishing, 364 Innovation Drive
North Clarendon, VT 05759-9436
Tel: 1 (802) 773 8930; Fax: 1 (802) 773 6993
Email: info@tuttlepublishing.com
www.tuttlepublishing.com

Japan
Tuttle Publishing, Yaekari Building, 3rd Floor
5-4-12 Ōsaki, Shinagawa-ku, Tokyo 141-0032
Tel: (81) 3 5437 0171; Fax: (81) 3 5437 0755
Email: sales@tuttle.co.jp
www.tuttle.co.jp

Asia Pacific
Berkeley Books Pte. Ltd., 3 Kallang Sector, #04-01,
Singapore 349278
Tel: (65) 67412178; Fax: (65) 67412179
Email: inquiries@periplus.com.sg
www.tuttlepublishing.com

24 23 22 21   11 10 9   2112MP
Printed in Singapore

TUTTLE PUBLISHING® is a registered trademark of
Tuttle Publishing, a division of Periplus Editions (HK) Ltd.

Contents

Appendices

Foreword

After twenty years of practice, Professor Cheng Man-ch'ing in 1950 published *Cheng-tzu T'ai-chi Ch'uan Shih-san P'ien* (Cheng's Thirteen Chapters on T'ai-chi Boxing). A decade later the growing popularity of T'ai-chi Ch'uan in the world led Cheng to publish a text in English on the art. The text suffered, however, from severe inadequacies in scope and presentation. At Cheng's request, I took the text to the present publisher, but he was as disturbed about its imperfections as I. He suggested a fresh start on an entirely new book with my full collaboration. The present book is the result. It has been built from the published versions of Cheng's two books—the one in Chinese and the other in English—as well as from the oral instructions in T'ai-chi that I received from Cheng and my own research concerning the art.

Cheng Man-ch'ing is a remarkable man. He is a versatile and brilliant master of the "Five Excellences" (Painting, Poetry, Calligraphy, Medicine, and T'ai-chi), on the wrong side of sixty, but with the vitality of a man much younger. After I knocked on his door for a year—the usual Chinese custom—he accepted me as a student. For more than seven years it has been my pleasure to learn the intricacies of the art under his tutelage. Every bit a gentleman, he is the living representation of T'ai-chi. I have studied many systems of T'ai-chi and have had the opportunity to see in action the leading teachers of Taiwan, Hong Kong, and Singapore. None can stand before Cheng.

So in all sincerity let it be said: this is his book. My part in it is to present his teaching as clearly as possible. Paraphrasing Michael Drayton speaking of his beloved Wales, I wish to say of T'ai-chi: "If I have not done it right, the want is in my ability, not in my love."

Both Professor Cheng and I thank Liu Chen-huan for his diligent efforts in helping to put the manuscript in final form;

E. Gunberg, B. Fusaro, and D. Slater for editorial corrigenda and suggestions; and W. Neisler, R. Mischke, and E. Maginnes for assistance with the graphics. And by no means least, we thank Sylvia Jackson for her patient and excellent typing of the text through several revisions.

ROBERT W. SMITH

CHAPTER ONE

Introducing T'ai-chi

Man cannot live fully without exercise. The *I Ching* (Book of Changes) says: "Nature is always in motion. Man also should strengthen himself without interruption." Exercise leads to robust health, high spirits, and rational thinking. There are, however, many kinds of exercise: ballplaying, swimming, traditional boxing, wrestling, and weightlifting, to name but a few. Without exception, each has built-in limitations. Weather restricts ballplaying, weakness prevents participation in the more rigorous sports, and age and sex inhibit activity in others. More importantly, though these sports differ in form, they are similar in that most never go beyond reliance on weight, force, and speed.

T'ai-chi is both an integrated exercise and an enjoyable sport for all: rich and poor, strong and weak, young and old, male and female. Weather does not inhibit its practice. Requirements of time and space are minimal. If one has a space approximately four feet on a side and can spare ten minutes a day, he can practice T'ai-chi without spending a cent.

For hundreds of years Westerners have been puzzled at seeing Chinese from all walks of life doing this effortless, rhythmical, ballet-like exercise both at dawn and at dusk. By way of explanation, Chinese say that whoever practices T'ai-chi, correctly and regularly, twice a day over a period of time will gain the pliability of a child, the health of a lumberjack, and the peace of mind of a sage. The amazing results achieved suggest that this is not just idle boasting, that perhaps, in some way unknown to Western science, T'ai-chi can indeed do all this, and more. Stressing slow respiration and balanced, relaxed postures, it certainly promotes deep breathing, digestion, the functioning of the internal organs, and blood circulation. And perhaps there is also basis for the claim that T'ai-chi can relieve, if not actually cure, neurasthenia, high blood pressure, anemia, tuberculosis, and many other maladies.

The T'ai-chi symbol and the eight trigrams. T'ai-chi's eight postures as well as the functions of evolution and the operations of nature are symbolized by the eight trigrams.

Besides the Solo Exercise (pages 12–77) with its therapeutic value, T'ai-chi also has two other aspects. The Pushing-Hands Practice (pages 80–89), in which two opponents compete in trying to uproot each other, constitutes a sport. Beyond this, T'ai-chi is a method of self-defense par excellence. Judo, Aikido, and a few other Asian methods stress the yielding principle of T'ai-chi, but none achieve to the same degree its relaxation, suppleness, and subtlety.

The Taoists advocate *wu wei* (non-action or effortlessness) and the Buddhists venerate "emptying." The motto for T'ai-chi practice must be "investment in loss." It is what Confucius meant by *k'e chi*—to subdue the self. How is this manifested in mundane affairs? It means to yield to others, thus quashing obstinacy, egotism, and selfishness. But it is not an easy thing. To persist in the Solo Exercise amid life's busy requirements is self-humbling. In the Pushing-Hands Practice, the student must accept failure many times over in the early stages. To yield and adhere to an opponent cannot be achieved by an egotist—his ego will not tolerate the bruisings necessary before mastery comes. But here, as in life, this proximity to reality must overcome ego if one is to walk a whole man.

THE NAME   The full and formal title is T'ai-chi Ch'uan (pronounced "tie-jee chwan,") the latter word meaning simply "fist" or "boxing." The term *t'ai-chi*

Yang Cheng-fu, a late master of T'ai-chi. Yang was the teacher who handed down this centuries-old art to the senior author. He is the author of "Yang Cheng-fu's Twelve Important Points" (see Chapter VII).

is derived from a concept of Chinese philosophy meaning "supreme ultimate." Philosophically, T'ai-chi is said to be the primary principle of all things and is represented by a circle divided into light and dark aspects, representing the yang and yin concepts, which reflect opposite attributes such as male and female, activity and inactivity, firmness and softness, light and darkness, and positive and negative. Through the complementary interaction of yin and yang sprang the five elements—fire, water, earth, wood, and metal. This book is not the place to go into the intricacies of the subject. Suffice it to say that T'ai-chi was named for an ultimate philosophical principle because its early proponents felt it expressed an ultimate physical principle.

HISTORY   There are four main theories on the origin of T'ai-chi. The most popular states that Chang San-feng, a Taoist priest of the Yuan dynasty (1279–1368), learned it in a dream.* A second theory holds that it originated in the T'ang dynasty (618–907) and developed

* Legend sits heavily on this personage: he was reputed to have lived several hundred years and his exploits were so supernormal that one must conclude that they derive more from legend than from historical fact. His more responsible biographers and his tombstone state simply that Chang was a Taoist living on Mt. Wutang in Hupeh province and that he created a so-called internal school of boxing. The postures of his method, however, bear little resemblance to the T'ai-chi we know today.

through four separate schools: the Hsu, Yu, Ch'eng, and Yin. A third claim states that the Ch'en family of Ch'en Chia Kou in Honan province created T'ai-chi during the Ming dynasty (1368–1654). The fourth thesis—and the most reasonable— simply avers that the founder is unknown, but that the development of T'ai-chi dates from one Wang Tsung-yueh of Shansi province, who introduced it in Honan during the reign of Ch'ien-lung (1736–95) of the Ch'ing dynasty. This last theory holds that once, while passing through Ch'en Chia Kou in Wen-hsien (Honan province), Wang Tsung-yueh saw the villagers practicing a form of hand boxing called *pao ch' ui.* Later at his inn he made an offhand remark on the method, which the villagers—almost all surnamed Ch'en— had practiced for generations. His remark brought several challenges and he met them all successfully. The villagers were impressed and asked Wang to stay for a short while to teach them his method. Moved by their sincerity, he agreed and helped them modify their hard boxing method into the softer T'ai-chi.

Much later, T'ai-chi at Ch'en Chia Kou was divided into the "new" and "old" styles, with Ch'en Ch'ang-hsing representing the "old" and Ch'en Yu-pen the "new." Ch'en Chiang-hsiang, another famed teacher of the "old" style, was engaged by a druggist in Yung Lien Hsien (in what is now Hopei province) to teach his sons. A servant of the family, Yang Lu-ch'an, secretly watched the practices and soon became so expert he was accepted as a student. Yang later went to Peking, capital of the Ch'ing dynasty, where he taught the emperor's guards. He met challenges from all sides of the boxing spectrum and was never defeated.

Yang Lu-ch'an passed his art on to his two sons, Chien-hou (d. 1917) and Pan-hou (d. 1881). Chien-hou in turn transmitted the family skill to his two sons, Shao-hou (d. 1929) and Cheng-fu (d. 1935). The latter, Yang Cheng-fu, brought T'ai-chi of the Yang variety to South China.* The author of this present text, Cheng Man-ch'ing, learned personally from Yang for nearly a decade and today is spreading the Yang style of T'ai-chi throughout the world.

---

* See Chapter VII for the core of Yang Cheng-fu's teaching.

CHAPTER TWO

Principles of T'ai-chi

RELAXATION AND CH'I In considering the fundamental principles of T'ai-chi we immediately come upon a word—*ch'i* (pronounced "chee")—which is as important as it is difficult to define. It can mean simply "air," as in the context of respiration, but in true T'ai-chi it should mean much more. W. T. Chan has well observed that "ch'i denotes the psychophysiological power associated with blood and breath," or another English equivalent might be "intrinsic energy." Oddly enough, most writers in English on T'ai-chi have maintained an embarrassed silence concerning *ch'i*. Cheng Man-ch'ing, however, gives it a central place in his system, saying that mind *(i)* and intrinsic energy *(ch'i)* are complementary bases of T'ai-chi, without which it would become merely a physiological exercise undeserving of the name "supreme ultimate." In the present book, then, *ch'i* is considered to be at the very heart of T'ai-chi, and we shall continue to use the Chinese term rather than any of the necessarily inexact English equivalents.

How should a novice begin his training in T'ai-chi? He should relax completely. The aim is to throw every bone and muscle of the body wide open so that the *ch'i* may travel unobstructed. Once this is done, the chest must be further relaxed and the *ch'i* made to sink to the navel. After a time the *ch'i* will be felt accumulating for mass integration in the navel, from where it will begin to circulate throughout the body. A tornado is but the massed movement of air and a tidal wave that of water. As a whiff, nothing is more pliable than air; as a drop, nothing more yielding than water. But as tornadoes and tidal waves, air and water carry everything before them. Mass integration makes the difference. Later, the student will be able to direct the *ch'i* instantaneously to any part of his body by means of his mind.

Exercise your spine so that the *ch'i* can travel this avenue to the top of your head. Your head is held as if suspended by the scalp from the ceiling of the room. This posture immobilizes the head and spine so that neither can move independently of the rest of the body. It strengthens the spine, the vital inner organs, and the brain itself. Make a habit of concentrating on the *ch'i*. This can be done at work or play, walking or riding. Formation of the habit requires perseverance but is infinitely better and far less expensive than the modern practice of regular ingestion of medicines.

The movement deriving from this internal generation and circulation of the *ch'i* we call "propelled" movement. During the exercise, limbs and other body components are moved

You must become like a child.

not so much by localized exertions as by the force of the *ch'i*. In the next, more advanced stage, the *ch'i* is absorbed by and stored in the marrow, causing the bones to become steel hard and essentially indestructible. When this stage is accomplished the student may be said to have reached the highest level.

LIKE A CHILD   Observe a child. Note how he breathes —not high in the chest but low in the abdomen. See, too, how he meets an accident—relaxed and with no apprehension in his mind. You may charge this off to ignorance, but, this notwithstanding, the child more often than not emerges from accidents unscathed. So perhaps the experience/intelligence clogging the adult's mind and causing his body to stiffen is really not such an asset after all. Let the child grasp your finger and try to retract it. Difficult, isn't it? The grasp is firm but not frenzied; there is true energy involved. Finally, watch how a child stands —straight but not stiff. We can truly learn from children. T'ai-chi believes that progress can be made only if one becomes like a child.

CHAPTER THREE

T'ai-chi for a Healthier Life

The chief aim of this book is to impart information on T'ai-chi as a system of health-giving exercises. This chapter gives the information which is required by the reader before he begins the exercises in the following chapter. The application of T'ai-chi in sport and self-defense is presented in Chapters V and VI.

THE THREE FACTORS In T'ai-chi three factors are very important: correct teaching, perseverance, and natural talent. Of the three, correct teaching (or right method) is the most important. Without it, no success comes even if a student of high natural ability works himself beyond human endurance. On the other hand, given the right kind of instruction, success can be achieved through perseverance even if one's natural talent is below average. In essence, two of the three factors—correct teaching and perseverance—are prerequisites for success. Natural ability is only helpful when the other factors are also present. There is a wonderful passage in Confucius which says: "Some are born with knowledge, some derive it from study, and some acquire it only after a painful realization of their ignorance. But the knowledge being possessed, it comes to the same thing. Some study with a natural ease, some from a desire for advantages, and some by strenuous effort. But the achievement being made, it comes to the same thing."*

The usual type of T'ai-chi consists of 128 postures, including many repetitions. To go through a full round requires more than fifteen minutes if done at the recommended speed. In order to shorten the time required, Cheng Man-ch'ing reduced the number of postures to thirty-seven by eliminating most of the repeated postures. Compared with

* *The Doctrine of the Mean*

the earliest T'ai-chi, which numbered only thirteen postures, Cheng's method contains nearly triple the number of the original actions. Moreover, it does not leave out any of the essential elements of the 128-posture method nor does it change the sequence. To go through a round requires from three to five minutes, depending on one's speed. If done daily, one round in the morning before breakfast and one before retiring at night will contribute greatly to a healthy life. This ten-minute investment a day is paltry enough, but the returns are great. The student, however, must take care not to miss a round. Miss a meal, be a few minutes late for bed, but don't miss a round of T'ai-chi. Perseverance is a must!

If one has natural talent, his progress will of course be speedier and surer. Unfortunately, in this respect nature is liberal to some and sparing to others. Moreover, when the allotment is made, it is fixed and beyond human power to modify it for the better. Knowledge and skill are quite different—even the least talented can acquire these through determined application. In *The Doctrine of the Mean* Confucius speaks thus of the superior man and learning: "He will not interrupt his labor. If another succeeds by one effort, he will use a hundred; if another succeeds by ten efforts, he will use a thousand. If a man proceeds in this way, though dull, he will surely become intelligent; though weak, he will surely become strong." Therefore, if lacking in natural aptitude, do not despair. All that is required is more work!

MOVEMENT   All movements are done with a relaxed body and a calm but concentrated mind. Walk like a cat—light and firm. In moving backward, touch the toe down first; in going forward, let the heel touch first. Then, as you shift your weight onto the foot, let the rest of the sole gradually proceed into place. Make the hands and head move as a part of the body and not independently. Almost all the movements are made circularly. This permits the reserving of energy, negates tension, and enhances relaxation, quite apart from its functional benefits. From Posture 3 to the concluding posture of the Solo Exercise (with the exception of Postures 24 and 33-I) the level of the body remains generally the same, that is, there is no rise and fall from shifts of body weight and there is little squatting or bending at the waist.

SLOWNESS The movements must be done at the same slow pace throughout. There are no fast postures—all are done at the same speed. The student may vary the speed used for the entire round, but he should not vary the speed of separate postures. Slowness permits distinctness of movement and is attuned to calmness of mind. Also, it enables the mind to function to its fullest in imagining an opponent and in recognizing and appreciating the role played by the components of the body as one moves through the exercise.

SWIMMING IN AIR Man lives on land. His long familiarity with air often makes him forget its existence. Since it lacks solidity and shape, it eludes attention or easy mental grasp by the beginner. To liken air to water aids the imagination. It is like water in the sense that if one pretends to swim while out of water, his movements automatically conform to the principles of T'ai-chi. By this practice, the novice ultimately will "feel" the air to be heavy in the sense that he feels water to be heavy. At this stage his body has become lighter and more pliable than that of the average man. This feeling of buoyancy and suppleness derives from firmly rooting the feet and using the body in "dry swimming." Functionally, this slow movement against an imagined resistance will ultimately create great speed in responding to a fighting situation.

LINKAGE Although the movements are done slowly, there is no interruption. The postures flow evenly without pause from start to end. The *ch'i* is blocked when the flow is impeded. Once one has paused, it takes several postures before one is again "on the track." This wastes these postures since, if they are not *true,* they are useless. Do the exercises as though "pulling silk from a cocoon." Although Westerners initially may not understand this, a few words will make it clear. In pulling silk one must pull slowly, easily, and—above all—steadily. If one pauses, the strand will break when the pulling is started again.

TRANQUILLITY Slowing down the natural processes will not help if the mind is not calmed. Eschew routine thoughts; initially concentrate on the postures. At first it will be difficult to block out extraneous thoughts and images, but disciplined practice will prevail in the end. As you proceed through the postures, you must think totally on them, so totally, in fact, that the mind literally embraces the postures and vice versa.

BREATHING Correct breathing must be coordinated with your movements. Inhale through your nose as you extend your arms outward or upward and exhale through your nose as you contract your arms or bring them downward. Initially, it is best not to be too concerned about breathing: first learn the techniques of the postures and then incorporate the breathing. Ultimately, the breathing becomes such an intrinsic part of the exercise that you will not even have to think of it.

You are now ready to begin to learn the physical-exercise aspect of T'ai-chi, the Solo Exercise. Remember, as you are learning the exercises, to strive to form good habits based on the principles you have learned in this chapter.

CHAPTER FOUR

The Solo Exercise

This section is the focal point of the book. Pains have been taken to make the explanatory material—both text and graphics—as clear as possible. Study it, work with it, and knowledge will come.

The entire Solo Exercise consists of sixty-five postures; thirty-seven are basic postures and twenty-eight are repetitions of basic postures. Each posture is designated by a number and name. For example, Posture 12, Brush Left Knee and Twist Step; followed by Posture 13, Play the Guitar. Following these is Posture 13A, which is a repetition of the movements in Posture 12.

Photographs for each posture are placed next to the appropriate text and are numbered consecutively for easy reference. *All the photographs in this chapter are printed in reverse image* to facilitate imitation of the movements illustrated. Thus you should follow the photographs exactly as though you were looking at your own reflection in a mirror.

Accompanying each photograph is a diagram showing the exact position and weighting of the feet. North is always toward the top of the page. Note that *these foot diagrams are not reversed* and hence show the position of your own feet as you stand looking in the "mirror" of the photographs. A key to the eight types of weightings indicated in the diagrams is given at the end of the book.

Also on the same page is the Sequence Diagram of the Solo Exercise. Again north is at the top of the page. This diagram will provide additional orientation as you begin to link together the various postures. It will also serve as a sort of shorthand guide after you have mastered the postures and begin to practice the full exercise as the uninterrupted sequence it should be.

POSTURE 1

Preparation

Yu-pei Shih

Stand erect facing north, your heels together *(Photo 3)*. Shift your weight to your right leg, bend it slightly, and rest on it. Raise your left foot and place it about a foot laterally to the left, your toes pointing directly forward. Shift most of your weight to this foot. Turn your right foot on its heel inward until it is parallel with your left foot. Both feet should point directly ahead and your knees should be bent slightly. The distance between your feet should equal the width of your shoulders. Bend your elbows slightly outward and the backs of your wrists upward. Your fingertips are raised slightly and are relaxed, neither stretched nor clenched (see page 68 for T'ai-chi hand). Your palms are down. Hold your head erect, your shoulders slumped, and your chest depressed, enabling your *ch'i* to sink to your navel. Your tongue should be held against the hard palate (roof of the mouth) and your mouth lightly closed. Without staring, look directly ahead *(4)*. Your mind is at ease and concentrates calmly on your breathing.

5 6 7

Beginning

Ch'i Shih

Inhaling slowly, raise your arms upward to shoulder height. The wrists should be bent, the fingers hanging down, until your arms reach the height of your shoulders *(Photo 5)*. Then, as you mobilize your *ch'i,* extend your fingers *(6)*. Your arms should ascend almost as if they were raised from above by something outside of yourself. Now draw back your arms by bending your elbows and, when your hands near your chest, lightly take them to your sides, fingers down, your wrists carried as though sinking into water and your fingertips floating off *(7)*. You are again in the position ending Posture 1.

Grasp Sparrow's Tail, Ward-off, Left

Lan Ch'iao Wei, P'eng, Tso

Shifting most of your weight to your left leg, bend your knee, relax the right side of your upper torso, and turn on your right heel, toes raised slightly, to the direct right (east). The bending of the left knee lowers the body; one knee or the other is kept well bent through the remainder of the Solo Exercise until the concluding posture. Your right foot is now at right angles to your left foot. In turning, you must move your waist and thigh coincidentally with your foot. Simultaneously, raise your right hand, palm down, to the level of your right armpit, and your left hand, palm up, to the right side of your waist. Thus you simulate holding a ball in your hands. Be careful to keep your right shoulder slumped and relaxed during this action. Your eyes accompany the movement and now look directly to the right. Your weight has shifted to your right foot, so that your left is brought to its toes *(Photo 8)*. Now, take a step directly north with your left foot, the heel touching first. Bending your left knee, gradually shift 70 percent of your weight to your left foot while turning the right side of your upper torso to the left. Raise your left hand to a point parallel with your chest, palm toward you and slightly down. Simultaneously, lower your right hand beside your right thigh. Lastly, turn your right foot on its heel slightly inward. Your eyes accompany the gradual turn and now look directly north *(9)*. Grasp Sparrow's Tail comprises the four movements: Ward-off, Rollback, Press, and Push.

10   11

POSTURE 4

Grasp Sparrow's Tail, Ward-off, Right

Lan Ch'iao Wei, P'eng, Yu

Shift most of your weight to your left leg until your right foot is brought to its toes. Simultaneously, turn your left hand over so that the palm is down while your right palm is up *(Photo 10)*. Relaxing your left shoulder, turn your right thigh to the right, turn on your right toes about 45°, and take your right foot four inches forward from its previous position and place it down heel first at the spot previously occupied by the toe. Shift 70 percent of your weight to your bent right leg. Your upper torso is now in the Ward-off, Right posture. Your right arm, with its palm toward your chest, has the elbow slightly down, and your left arm, elbow down, has its palm facing outward midway between your right wrist and elbow, but not touching. Lastly, stretch your left leg and turn your left foot slightly inward by turning on the heel *(11)*. You now face directly east.

12   13

POSTURE 5

Grasp Sparrow's Tail, Rollback

Lan Ch'iao Wei, Lu

Relax your right arm, turn your upper torso to the right (southeast), and extend your right arm slightly *(Photo 12)*. Then turn your right wrist simultaneously with your waist to the northeast while your left hand, palm up, is held near your right elbow for protection. Your left knee is bent and receives all your weight as your upper torso and arms turn back to the northeast *(13)*. This posture is the epitome of the yielding required in T'ai-chi and must be done correctly. Remember that your arms do not move independently of your body.

POSTURE 6

Grasp Sparrow's Tail, Press

Lan Ch'iao Wei, Chi

Continuing, carry your left hand in a clockwise circle, turn your right hand so the palm faces your chest, and protect your chest with your right arm, elbow bent. The fingers of your left hand lightly touch your right arm between your elbow and wrist. Stretch your left leg and shift 70 percent of your weight to your right leg. Press forward and slightly upward, keeping your arms relaxed *(Photo 14)*. You are now facing directly east again.

14

Grasp Sparrow's Tail, Push

Lan Ch'iao Wei, An

Withdraw, shifting all of your weight again to your left foot while separating your hands, which come in front of your shoulders, the palms facing outward *(Photo 15)*. Then shift 70 percent of your weight forward to your right leg and push forward with both arms and upper torso *(16)*. Your arms are bent but do not move except as part of your body. If they act independently, the exercise is worthless. This rule applies to every posture. Heed it well.

15　　　　　　　　　　　　　　　　**16**

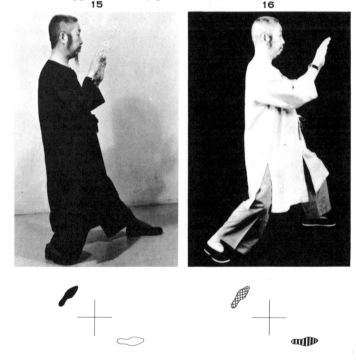

17   18   19

POSTURE 8

Single Whip

Tan Pien

Shifting most of your weight to your left foot, turn on your right heel and turn the toes inward as far as possible. Simultaneously, holding your arms parallel and slightly bent at the elbows, turn your body as far as possible to the rear left corner (northwest) *(Photo 17)*. Now, as you shift most of your weight back to your right leg, bring your left palm up near your right armpit. At the same time, your right hand circles laterally, counterclockwise in front of your chest and then makes a hook with the fingers pointing down above your left palm. Raise your left heel and turn the foot a little to the left (by bringing the heel rightward) while extending your right "hook" hand to the right corner (northeast), relaxed and not rigid *(18)*. Now, take a big step to the front left with your left foot, the heel touching first. Gradually shift your weight to your left leg and bend the knee. Simultaneously, extend your left hand, palm inward, at chest level to the left until your waist faces directly west. Then turn your palm up and outward as your eyes, which have accompanied the gradual turn, look out over your fingers. Lastly, turn on your right heel and turn the toes inward *(19)*. Make this a big stretching movement but keep your spine straight, your navel facing straight ahead, and don't let your left knee extend beyond your left toes.

20

POSTURE 9

Lift Hands

T'i Shou

Turn your upper torso slightly to the right and shift almost all of your weight to your left leg. Resting on your left leg, bring your right foot leftward to where it comes down lightly on the heel, the knee bent. Your right foot is now on a line with your left heel. Relax your arms and turn them inward so that the palms face each other. Slowly bring your arms closer together until your right hand is in front, aligned with your right leg, and your left hand in back directly opposite your right elbow. Both your arms are bent and the backs of your wrists bowed *(Photo 20)*.

As you bring your right foot back near your left heel and put it down on the toes, bring your arms back, your right hanging beside your right thigh and your left near your abdomen *(Photo 21)*. Now, step forward with your right foot and shift 70 percent of your weight to it. Your right hand protects your groin and your left hand is held near the middle of your right forearm. Your right shoulder leans slightly forward as you face north *(22)*. Remember to shift your weight gradually and smoothly; this is facilitated by putting your heel down first and letting the remainder of the foot follow.

21   22

23

POSTURE 11

Stork Spreads Wings

Pai-hao Liang Ch'ih

Turn to the left (west) and raise your right arm in a small circle inside your left up to where your right elbow parallels your chin and your right hand stretches to a point above your right ear. Simultaneously, lower your left hand beside your left thigh. Almost all your weight is on your right foot as you bring your left foot forward diagonally right and put only the toes down on a line with your right heel *(Photo 23)*.

24   25

Posture 12

Brush Left Knee and Twist Step

Tso Lou Hsi Yao Pu

With your weight still on your right foot, turn slightly to your right and lower your right hand beside your right thigh while your left hand circles clockwise down past your chest and stops by your left thigh. Your left foot comes flush to the ground but carries no weight *(Photo 24)*. Step forward with your left foot slightly to the diagonal left, the heel touching first. Shift 70 percent of your weight forward to your left foot. Simultaneously, bring your right hand under your right ear and circle it forward while your left palm brushes near your left knee and stops outside it *(25)*. Lastly, turn your right foot slightly inward by pivoting on your heel. You still face west.

26   27   28

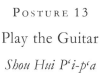

POSTURE 13

Play the Guitar

Shou Hui P'i-p'a

Shift more of your weight forward to your left leg. Raise your right foot from the floor, turn it 30° to the right, put it down toes first, and shift all your weight to it. While bringing your right hand back, raise your left hand so that the fingers are aligned with your face. Your right hand should now be opposite your left elbow. Simultaneously, your left foot takes a half step directly right, only your heel touching the ground. This posture simulates playing a guitar *(Photo 26)*.

POSTURE 13A

Repetition of Posture 12, Brush Left Knee and Twist Step, in the same direction *(27–28)*.

29

There are several movements in Posture 14 representing one distinct technique. Following the preceding posture, withdraw your body, shifting almost all your weight to your right foot, and place your right palm beside your left thigh. Turn on your left heel and place the toes down three inches to the left, and then shift most of your weight to your left foot *(Photo 29)*. Take a full step to the diagonal forward right with your right foot and put it down, the toes pointing northwest *(30)*. Gradually shift your weight to your right foot. Make a light fist (see page 68 for T'ai-chi fist) with your right hand and carry it, knuckles down, to your right side. At the same time, your left hand circles beside your left ear and chops lightly forward. Next, step forward with your left foot, heel touching first and toes straight ahead *(31)*. Shift 70 percent of your weight to it. Your right fist

30

31

32

follows the movement of your waist and left leg and strikes forward below your left wrist *(32)*. The chop and punch should be done slowly and without force.

POSTURE 15

Withdraw and Push

Ju Feng Ssu Pi

The literal translation of this posture is "Apparent Closure," but because this is functionally meaningless it has been retitled in English. From the preceding posture, open your right fist and bring it back near your left shoulder as your left arm is brought up outside your right, forming an X. Both palms face your chest. Bring both arms closer to your chest and shift most of your weight to your right foot *(Photo 33)*. Separate your hands, turn the palms out, and push forward as you shift 70 percent of your weight ahead to your left leg *(34)*.

33   34

35   36

POSTURE 16

Cross Hands

Shih-tzu Shou

Shift most of your weight to your right foot and
turn your body to the right (north) with your right
arm carried in a high circle clockwise and your left
arm following your waist *(Photo 35)*. At the same
time, turn on your left heel and turn the toes inward
facing north. Next, shift most of your weight to
your left leg as your left hand describes a smaller
circle than your right and is brought inside your
right arm, both forming an X. Simultaneously, draw
your right foot rearward until it is on a line with
your left foot, both feet pointing directly ahead.
Both feet are under your shoulders as in Posture 2,
Beginning, but now all of your weight rests on your
left foot *(36)*. Both knees are well bent.

Embrace Tiger and Return to Mountain

Pao Hu Kuei Shan

Turn your waist to the right rear (southeast) and separate your hands. Your right hand goes outside your right thigh as your left hand, palm down, passes near your left ear. Simultaneously, take a big step with your right foot to the right rear (southeast) and shift 70 percent of your weight to it. After your right hand brushes the right knee, turn the palm up. At the same time stretch your left hand, palm down, to the right (southeast) and look directly over it. Lastly, turn on your left heel, so that your foot is slightly inward and aligned with the direction in which you face *(Photo 37)*.

37

38   39   40

POSTURE 17A

Repetition of Posture 5, Grasp Sparrow's Tail, Rollback, but done facing southeast rather than east *(Photos 38–39)*.

POSTURE 17B

Repetition of Posture 6, Grasp Sparrow's Tail, Press, but done facing southeast rather than east *(40)*.

POSTURE 17C

Repetition of Posture 7, Grasp Sparrow's Tail, Push, but done facing southeast rather than east *(41–42)*.

POSTURE 17D

Substantially a repetition of Posture 8, Single Whip, but done facing northwest rather than west *(43–45)*.

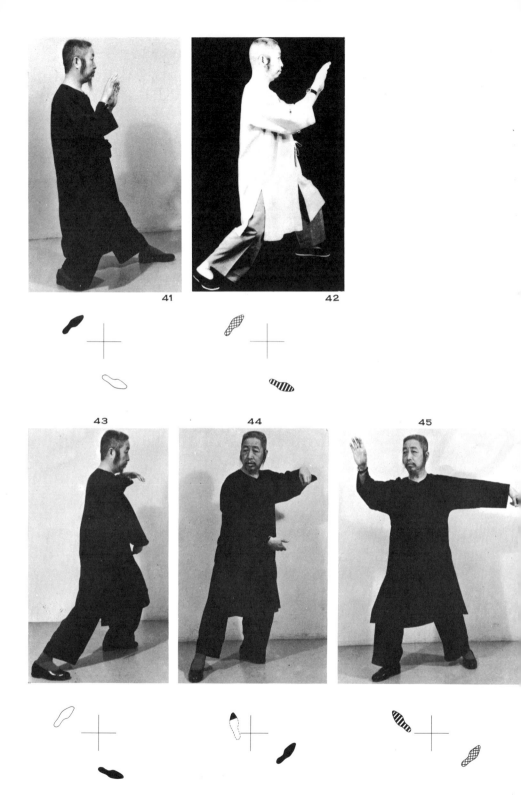

41   42

43   44   45

46

47

POSTURE 18

Punch Under Elbow

Chou Ti K'an Ch'ui

Draw back and shift most of your weight to your right foot. Take a step with your left foot to the left (west) and shift your weight to it. At the same time, open your right "hook" hand, turn your upper torso to the left, and bring your right foot forward, your toes on a line with your left heel and pointing northwest. Shift most of your weight to your right foot as your torso continues swinging leftward with both arms evenly spaced *(Photo 46)*. When you have turned as far as you can and your right hand is near your left shoulder, your left hand circles near your chest inside your right arm and ends vertically, fingers before your eyes. At the same time take a half step with your left foot diagonally to the center front, only the heel touching, and make a fist with your right hand, which cups your left elbow *(47)*.

48   49

POSTURE 19

Step Back and Repulse Monkey, Right

Tao Nien Hou, Yu

Open your right fist and draw it back, palm up, past
your right side near your right ear and turn the palm
down. At the same time extend your left hand, palm
down, to the front. As you turn your left palm up
(Photo 48), step slightly diagonally to your left rear
with your left foot and place it down toes first, so
that it points straight ahead (west). Shift your weight
to your left foot and turn your right toes inward so
that your feet are parallel. Lastly, take your right
fingers past your right ear and thrust directly forward,
as your left hand, palm up, is brought back to your
left side *(49)*.

50

Circle your left hand, palm down, toward your left ear. With your weight concentrated on your left foot *(Photo 50)*, step directly back with your right foot and place it down, toes first, pointing straight ahead (west). Take your left fingers past your left ear and thrust directly forward as your right hand, palm up, is brought back to your right side and your weight shifts to your right foot *(51)*. Keep your toes pointed straight ahead as you step back.

POSTURE 20A

This posture repeats Posture 19, Step Back and Repulse Monkey, Right, done in the same direction *(52–53)*. Unlike Posture 19, however, after you bring your left foot back, there will be no need to turn your right toes inward since the steps in this last move-

51

52

53

ment of a three-part sequence follow a parallel path —that is, your left toes point straight ahead as you step back.

POSTURE 21

Diagonal Flying

Hsieh Fei Shih

Turn your right palm up and put your hand beside your left thigh as you turn your left palm so that your hands simulate holding a ball *(Photo 54)*. All your weight is concentrated on your left foot. Take a big step with your right foot to the right rear (northeast), heel touching first, and gradually shift 70 percent of your weight to it. At the same time circle your right hand underneath your left armpit to your right rear, where it is extended palm up. Lastly, turn on your left heel 45° to the right, your waist accompanying the move, and lightly hold your left palm near your left knee. Your eyes look at your right fingers *(55)*.

54

55

56   57

POSTURE 22

Wave Hands in Clouds, Right

Yun Shou, Yu

Turn your right palm down and draw it back near your armpit. While turning your upper torso as far as possible to the right, turn your left palm up and hold it beside your right side under your right hand. Again your hands simulate holding a ball. Take a half step to the north with your left foot, all your weight concentrated on your right foot *(Photo 56)*. Circle your right hand, palm in, under your left arm, and turn your right toes leftward so that the feet are parallel. Carrying your left hand, palm in, at the level of your throat and your right hand, palm in, at the level of your navel *(57)*, turn left until your hands again simulate holding a ball by your left side. Then take a half step with your right foot to the left. Throughout the movement your upper torso should be erect and not inclined to either side.

Wave Hands in Clouds, Left

Yun Shou, Tso

This posture begins with the simulated holding of the ball at your left side, your left hand, palm down, on top and your right hand, palm up, below, and your weight concentrated on your left foot *(Photo 58)*. Circle your left hand, palm in, under your right arm and hold it at the level of your navel, as you carry your right hand, palm in, to the level of your throat *(59)*. Turn right until your hands simulate holding a ball, right hand on top, left hand below. As your weight shifts from your left foot to your right, take a half step to the left with your left foot.

58

59

POSTURE 23A

Repetition of Posture 22, Wave Hands in Clouds, Right, in the same direction *(Photos 60-61)*.

POSTURE 23B

This posture repeats only the beginning of Posture 23, Wave Hands in Clouds, Left, in which you simulate holding a ball at your left side. Your left hand should be above, your right hand below, and all your weight concentrated on your left foot *(62)*.

60

61

62

POSTURE 23C

From the preceding action, in which you hold an imaginary ball at your left side, step a little diagonally to the northeast with your right foot *(Photo 63)*. Now shift all your weight to it. Simultaneously, take your right hand in the same direction and form a "hook" hand with it *(64)*. The remainder of the movement is the same as Posture 8 and the direction is the same *(65)*.

63
64
65

POSTURE 24

Squatting Single Whip

Tan Pien Hsia Shih

Turn your right foot on its heel 25° to the right as
you draw back and lower your body so that you
almost sit on your right foot. Simultaneously, turn
your left foot 25° inward to the right and draw your
left hand back to your right thigh. Next, thrust your
left hand along your left leg and forward as you turn
on your left heel 50° to the left. Your right hand is
kept hooked to maintain stability *(Photo 66)*.

66

67

POSTURE 25

Golden Cock Stands on
One Leg, Right

Chin Chi Tu-li, Yu

As you thrust your left hand forward, turn your right foot on its heel 25° to the left, bend your left leg slightly, and shift your weight to it. As you begin to rise, drop your right hand beside your right thigh. Standing on your bent left leg, raise your right leg, knee bent, so that your toes point down. At the same time, raise your right arm and hold it vertically above your knee. Your left hand lightly touches your left thigh *(Photo 67)*.

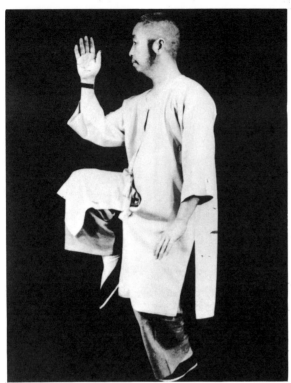

68

POSTURE 26

Golden Cock Stands on One Leg, Left

Chin Chi Tu-li, Tso

Put your right foot down a step rearward, toes touching first, and raise your bent left knee, toes pointing down. Simultaneously, raise your left hand inside your descending right hand and extend it vertically above your left knee. Your right hand ends up beside your right thigh *(Photo 68)*. Make sure your supporting leg, the right, is kept well bent.

Put your left foot down to the left rear and shift your weight to it. Simultaneously, turn your left palm up and lower it while you turn your upper torso south. Raise your right hand, palm in, to neck level and stretch it forward, palm down *(Photo 69)*. As you bring your right hand toward your chest, turn your left hand, palm down, and circle it clockwise above your right wrist to form an X in front of your chest. Turn your upper torso to the west. Retract your right foot, only the toes touching *(70)*. Next, separate your hands and kick lightly to the diagonal right (northwest) with the toes of your right foot. Keep your right foot straight. To maintain balance, your right arm is bent at the elbow, fingers extended upward *(71)*. In Postures 27 and 28 you must aim with your leg at an imaginary opponent's shin, kicking lightly.

69

70

71

72   73   74

POSTURE 28

Separate Left Foot

Tso Fen Chiao

Bring your right foot, still off the ground, back toward your left foot, put it down with the toes pointing northwest, and shift most of your weight to it.
Simultaneously, your right hand is brought back
near your chest. Take a short step with your left
foot to the southwest and extend your left arm
slightly, palm down, while your right hand, palm up,
is near your chest *(Photo 72)*. Bring your left foot
slightly toward you, only the toes touching, as you
circle your right hand counterclockwise above your
left hand to form an X, palms toward you *(73)*. Turning your palms outward, separate your hands, the left
striking forward to the diagonal left, the right held
to the rear of your head, as you kick lightly to the
southwest with the toes of your left foot *(74)*.

Turn and Strike with Heel

Chuan Shen Teng Chiao

Keeping your left foot off the ground, knee at waist level, toes down, retract it and your left hand *(Photo 75)*. Raising your right toes slightly, turn on your right heel to the left, the toes pointing south and your upper torso east. At the same time, circle your right hand counterclockwise until it joins the left wrist from outside *(76)*. Kick with your left heel directly forward (east) and chop forward above it with your left hand. Hold your right hand at head level, the fingers pointing up to sustain balance. This kick is different from the preceding ones (Postures 27 and 28) in that the heel, rather than the toes, is used as the striking member and the kick is focused higher. Your right leg should be bent, and your eyes should be looking over your left fingers *(77)*.

75   76   77

POSTURE 29A

Although this posture essentially repeats Posture 12, Brush Left Knee and Twist Step, it is done facing east instead of west, and is initiated from a different position. From the previous posture, withdraw your left foot, which has kicked forward. Next, take it diagonally forward to the left and put it down, the heel touching first. Simultaneously, bring your right hand under your right ear and circle it forward *(Photo 78),* while your left palm brushes near your left knee and stops outside it *(79).*

78 **79**

Brush Right Knee and Twist Step

Yu Lou Hsi Yao Pu

Although this is the first occurrence of the posture Brush Right Knee, the steps and weighting merely reverse those of three previous postures (12, 13A, and 29A). Shift your weight to your right foot. Now turn your left toes out 45°, shifting your weight to the left foot *(Photo 80)*. Next, step forward with your right foot, placing it down with the toes pointing directly ahead, but keep the weight on your left foot as you circle your left hand near your left ear. Your right hand hangs near your right inner thigh. As you shift 70 percent of your weight forward to your right foot, thrust straight ahead with your left hand, palm down, past your left ear as your right hand brushes near your right knee and comes to rest outside it *(81)*.

80   81

POSTURE 31

Step Forward and Strike with Fist

Chin-pu Tsai Ch'ui

Relax your waist and shift your weight to your left foot. Turn your right toes 45° to the right, clench your right fingers into a light fist, palm up, and hold it near your right thigh *(Photo 82)*. Simultaneously, draw your left palm back beside your right thigh and shift your weight to your right foot. Next, take a step forward with your left leg and shift 70 percent of your weight to it. Lastly, brush your left knee with your left hand and hold it outside the knee while your right fist strikes forward on a descending line *(83)*.

82 83

This posture is almost the same as Posture 4, Grasp Sparrow's Tail, Ward-off, Right, the direction being the same, but because of a forward step with the right foot—which was not a part of Posture 4—the instructions are repeated. Drawing back and shifting most of your weight to your right foot, turn your left foot on its heel so that the toes face 45° leftward. Shift most of your weight to your left foot and step forward with your right foot, your toes pointing directly ahead. Next, shift 70 percent of your weight to your right foot as your right arm rises, palm in, to the Ward-off posture, and your left hand, palm down, is pointed slightly upward near your right forearm *(Photo 84)*.

POSTURE 31B

Repetition of Posture 5, Grasp Sparrow's Tail, Rollback, in the same direction *(85-86)*.

84   85   86

| POSTURE 31C |

Repetition of Posture 6, Grasp Sparrow's Tail, Press, in the same direction *(Photo 87)*.

| POSTURE 31D |

Repetition of Posture 7, Grasp Sparrow's Tail, Push, in the same direction *(88–89)*.

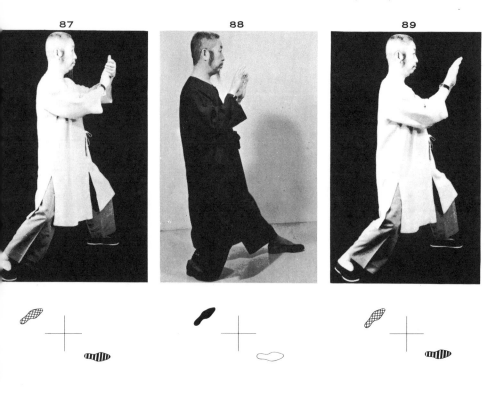

87 88 89

90   91   92

POSTURE 31E

Repetition of Posture 8, Single Whip, in the same direction *(Photos 90–92)*.

93

POSTURE 32

Fair Lady Works at Shuttles, Right

Yu Nu Ch'uan So, Yu

Draw back, shifting most of your weight to your right foot, and turn on your left heel as far as you can to the right. Now, shift most of your weight to your left foot. Your body accompanies the left foot in turning right and you now face northeast. Draw your left hand back under your right armpit as you open your right "hook" hand. Next, bring your right foot back slightly *(Photo 93)*. Shift most of your weight to it. Take a full step with your left foot to the northeast and shift 70 percent of your weight to it. At the same time slide your left hand, palm in, up your right forearm, and then turn it out across your forehead for protection. Lastly, press your right palm forward in a pushing motion while your right knee stretches slightly to add impetus *(94)*. The last action must be done primarily with the body, the right arm moving only as a part of the body.

94

Fair Lady Works at Shuttles, Left

Yu Nu Ch'uan So, Tso

Draw back and, turning on your heel, turn your left toes inward to the right as far as you can. Shift your weight to your left foot as you bring your right palm up and hold it under your left elbow *(Photo 95)*. This action will swing your right foot also to the right but without weight on it. Next, turn 180° to the right and take a full step further right with your right foot (from the starting position you have now turned 270°). Bend your right leg and shift 70 percent of your weight to it. Your right foot now points northwest. Sliding your right hand, palm in, up your left forearm, turn the palm out across your forehead for protection. Lastly, press your left palm forward in a pushing motion while your left knee stretches slightly to add impetus *(96)*.

95

96

97   98

POSTURE 33A

This posture repeats Posture 32, Fair Lady Works at Shuttles, Right, but because the direction is different a full explanation is given. Following the preceding posture, draw back and shift almost all your weight to your left foot. At the same time, turn your left palm upward and put it under your right elbow. Step two inches to the southwest with your right foot and put it down still facing northwest *(Photo 97)*. Shift most of your weight to your right foot. Next, turn 90° to your left (southwest) and step in that direction with your left foot. Shift 70 percent of your weight forward to your left foot as your left hand glides up your right forearm and ends by protecting the forehead, the palm out. Your right hand then pushes forward, its impetus enhanced by the stretching of your right leg *(98)*.

99   100

POSTURE 33B

This posture repeats Posture 33, Fair Lady Works at Shuttles, Left, but because the direction is different, a full explanation is given. Following the preceding posture, draw back and shift most of your weight to your right foot. Turn your left toes inward to the right as far as you can. Shifting most of your weight to your left foot *(Photo 99)*, turn your body 270° to the right (southeast) and take a step forward with your right foot. Shift 70 percent of your weight to your right foot. Your right hand, which has been held, palm up, under your left elbow, now rises up in front of your left forearm and protects your forehead. Lastly, push forward with your left hand as your left leg stretches to provide added impetus *(100)*.

101   102

| POSTURE 33C |

From the previous posture, bring both your hands
to your right side in the ball-holding position. Your
right hand, palm down, is above, and your left hand,
with the palm up, is below. Move your left foot a
few inches leftward, thus separating your legs *(Photo
101)*. Next, bending your left knee, gradually shift
70 percent of your weight to your left foot, at the
same time turning your upper torso to the left. Raise
your left hand to a point parallel with your chest,
palm toward you and slightly down. Simultaneously,
lower your right hand beside your right thigh and
turn your right foot on its heel slightly inward *(102)*.
This posture, although initiated from a different position, is a repeat of Posture 3, Grasp Sparrow's Tail,
Ward-off, Left, in the same direction.

103

POSTURE 33D

Repetition of Posture 4, Grasp Sparrow's Tail, Ward-off, Right, in the same direction *(Photos 103-4)*.

POSTURE 33E

Repetition of Posture 5, Grasp Sparrow's Tail, Rollback, in the same direction *(105-6)*.

104

105

106

POSTURE 33F

Repetition of Posture 6, Grasp Sparrow's Tail, Press, in the same direction *(Photo 107)*.

POSTURE 33G

Repetition of Posture 7, Grasp Sparrow's Tail, Push, in the same direction *(108-9)*.

107   108   109

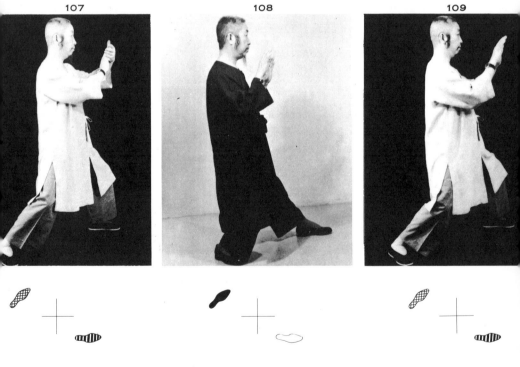

Repetition of Posture 8, Single Whip, in the same direction *(Photos 110–12)*.

110

111

112

POSTURE 33-I

Repetition of Posture 24, Squatting Single Whip, in the same direction *(Photo 113)*.

113

Step Forward to Seven Stars

Shang Pu Ch'i Hsing

As you rise, shift most of your weight to your left
foot and take a half step forward with your right
foot, only the toes touching the ground. Opening
your right "hook" hand, move it forward at the
same time that you move your right foot. When it
is in front of your chest, clench both hands into
fists and join them at the wrists, your left hand inside, your right hand outside *(Photo 114)*.

114

Step Back and Ride Tiger

T'ui Pu K'ua Hu

Opening your fists, take a full step to the rear with your right foot and shift your weight to it. Next, take a half step rearward with your left foot, only the toes touching the ground. Simultaneously, circle your right arm near your right shoulder, the forearm nearly vertical, stopping near your right ear, the fingers up, and the palm out. During this action, brush your left hand near your left knee *(Photo 115)*.

115

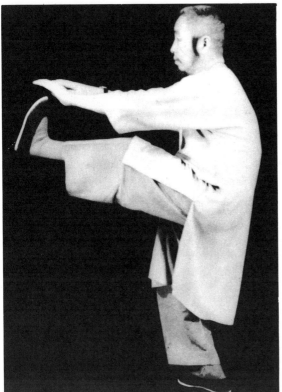

116

Stretching your left arm further left, circle your right hand to the left side of your waist. With your left heel already raised, lift your right heel slightly and turn your body a complete 360° turn to the right, most of your weight remaining on your right foot. Your right foot is on its toes and your arms are slightly extended forward and aligned with your shoulders. Next, shift your weight to your left foot and sweep your right leg in a rising clockwise circle, your toes slightly touching your palms, which are held at waist level *(Photo 116)*. Keep your right knee bent and don't slap downward on your right foot with your fingers but make your right foot come up to your palms.

Bend Bow and Shoot Tiger

Wan Kung She Hu

Bring your right leg, still clear of the ground, back to your left leg and then put it down pointing northwest. Slowly shift 70 percent of your weight to it. Move both hands simultaneously, the right palm out and left palm in, toward your right side. When your right hand reaches your right ear, your left hand is facing the left side of your chest. At this time make both hands into fists and carry them slightly forward, pointing directly west, the spaces between the thumb and index finger of each hand facing each other *(Photo 117)*. Your body must describe a circle going from left to right and then back slightly to the left.

117

118

POSTURE 37A

Raise your left foot and put it down a few inches to the rear, pointing southwest. Thereafter, this is a repetition of Posture 14, Step Forward, Deflect Downward, Parry, and Punch, in the same direction *(Photos 118–19).*

POSTURE 37B

Repetition of Posture 15, Withdraw and Push, in the same direction *(120–21).*

119

120

121

POSTURE 37C

Repetition of Posture 16, Cross Hands, in the same
direction *(Photos 122–23)*.

122   123

124

POSTURE 37D

Conclusion

Ho T'ai-chi

Relax, separate your arms and lower your hands to your sides. Shift half of your weight to your right foot—it is now shared equally by the two. As your hands descend to your sides, straighten your legs as in Posture 2, Beginning. This completes the Solo Exercise *(Photo 124)*. Now, check yourself against the Solo Exercise Checklist on page 68.

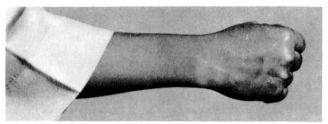

The T'ai-chi Fist

THE SOLO EXERCISE CHECKLIST

Did you . . .

1. Relax? ☐
2. Sink? ☐
3. Keep your sacrum plumb erect? ☐
4. Hold your head straight? ☐
5. Retain the "beauteous hand," straight but not stiff? ☐
6. Slump your shoulders? ☐
7. Depress your chest? ☐
8. Bend your knee(s)? ☐
9. Move slowly, gracefully, without interruption? ☐
10. Subordinate your arms to your body's movement? ☐
11. Breathe slowly, inhaling as your arms moved out, exhaling as your arms returned? ☐
12. Keep most of your weight on only one foot at time? ☐
13. Concentrate with an aware but easy mind? ☐

If you did . . . you have made an impressive start in learning the art of T'ai-chi.

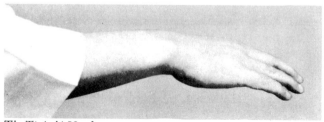

The T'ai-chi Hand

THE SOLO EXERCISE
A PHOTOGRAPHIC SEQUENCE

The following pages 70 to 77 are intended as a working
guide to the complete Solo Exercise. The purpose of
this arrangement is to present the overall pattern of
the postures in sequential order. It is hoped that this
linked arrangement will heighten your sense of the
flow of uninterrupted movement which is fundamental to the correct application of the Solo Exercise. The
Sequence Diagram (pp. 113-15), a directional guide
which shows the basic movements of the Solo Exercise, is intended as a complement ot this guide. Use
them in conjunction to achieve a more complete mastery of the important material you have already
learned.

*In keeping with the pattern of the entire Solo Exercise, the
photographs in this sequence are also shown in mirror image
and the foot-weighting diagrams correspond to the reader's
feet.*

POSTURE 1 POSTURE 2 POSTU

POSTURE 6 POSTURE 7 POSTURE 8

POSTURE 12 POSTURE 13

POSTURE 4   POSTURE 5

POSTURE 9   POSTURE 10   POSTURE 11

TURE 14   POSTURE 15

POSTURE 16   POSTURE 17

POSTURE 18   POSTURE 1

POSTURE 21   POSTURE 22   POSTURE

POSTURE 20

POSTURE 29 POSTURE 3

POSTURE 33

POSTURE 35   POSTURE 36   POSTURE 37

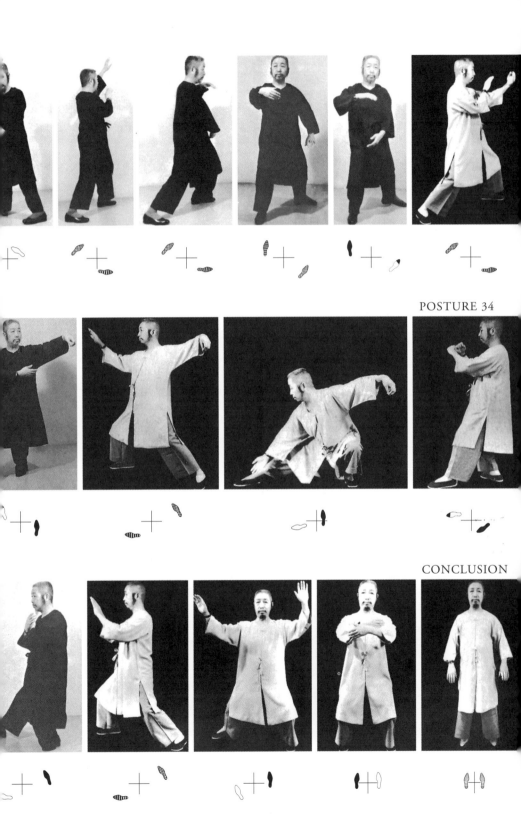

CHAPTER FIVE

T'ai-chi for Sport

Correct application of T'ai-chi hinges entirely on the mind. "To take advantage of impending motion and momentum" and "to deflect the impetus of a thousand pounds with a trigger force of four ounces" are statements in the *T'ai-chi Ch'uan Classics* emphasizing mental rather than physical ability. Traditional boxing, Western as well as Asian, combines muscular force, physical bravery, and technique. Without physical bravery and muscular force, mere technique avails little. T'ai-chi holds an entirely different view. As a sport or as an art of self-defense, it spurns both bravery and force. The *T'ai-chi Ch'uan Classics* tell us that "in any action the whole body must be made as light and mobile as possible." So light, in fact, that "the added weight of a feather will be felt, and so mobile that a fly cannot alight on it without setting it in motion."

In addition to the injunction to relax completely and to avoid using muscular force, the novice player is warned to "give himself up and yield before his opponent."* This sounds incredible to the orthodox boxer. To surrender one's body to full relaxation and to yield to the opponent—is this not courting disaster? But if the student fails to heed this advice he is certain to fail.

To illustrate, when a T'ai-chi expert meets an opponent who strikes at him, he neither resists nor counters the blow. Instead, he yields before the force, thus taking advantage of his opponent's momentum, and adds a pull or push so that with the augmented impetus the opponent, meeting no resistance, is thrown to the ground. This is how a mere four ounces can topple a thousand pounds. The four ounces do not defeat the thousand pounds, of course, but rather cause heavier force to defeat itself. This action exemplifies the

---

* This means to surrender the initiative to the opponent and to yield before him.

concept of "giving up oneself and yielding before the opponent."

By relaxing the body and by refusing to exert force or to tense one's muscles, mobility is enhanced, and this will deny the opponent any chance of getting across a telling blow—for there is no center of gravity for him to act upon. The limp fluidity of the defender provides no resistance point of the sort necessary for a knockout blow. This, however, is only a part of the reason that the T'ai-chi exponent is impervious to attack. Let us look again at the *Classics,* which assert that sound boxing is *"rooted in the feet, develops in the legs, is directed by the waist, and functions through the fingers."*

The feet must be firmly rooted. The *ch'i* develops the tensile spring of the legs as a source of strength. Strength is shot from the legs as an arrow is from a bow. The waist may be likened to the bow that directs the arrow. Philosopher Wang Yung-ming (1472–1528) wrote that the waist should be as pliable as if it were boneless. The waist directs the strength just as the bowstring does the arrow, determining its direction, range, and penetrating power. The *ch'i* develops (or sprouts) through the legs and waist and moves to the fingers. In other words, just as the force in an arrow extends from the bowstring to the arrow tip or head, the *ch'i* reaches from the feet to the fingertips.

The state of complete bodily relaxation has its roots in the feet. When the student is able to relax his body and root his feet, the boxing he then practices is called *nei-chia ch'uan* (the "internal"—as opposed to the "external"—system of boxing). This principle is illustrated by the weighted, broad-based Daruma doll of Japan, which sways at the slightest touch but which cannot be upended.

In T'ai-chi the weight is invariably put on one foot at a time. Except in the preliminary and closing postures, it is never shared between the two feet. To do so is a serious fault termed "double-weighting," which impedes agility and balance. The foot should be rooted like a tree with one tap-root. Of course the boxer has no tangible root connecting him to the ground, but, here again, over a period of time his mind can so assist this process that the student will feel as if his weight had actually penetrated the surface of the earth. His concentrated force will respond to gravity like iron to a magnet.

To speak of the foot taking root implies a concentration

of physical force in the foot, leaving none in the rest of the body. This is true. When the body is emptied of force—that is, when all the muscles are relaxed—a "tenacious strength" will develop from the foot. This tenacious strength is different from force in that it has a root, whereas force does not. In action, tenacity may be likened to a strong vine which is pliable, and force to a stick which is rigid. Tenacity is alive, force is inert. Tenacity is the resilience or tonicity of living muscles, however relaxed they may be. The muscles being relaxed, tenacity cannot involve the bones. Force, however, is derived from the tension of the muscles, binding the bones together in a wooden, rigid system.

Tradition says that "tenacity derives from muscles; force from bones." To strike with force requires the mobilization of the bones and the tensing of all the muscles so that the blow will be concentrated and fall like a mighty cudgel. To strike with tenacious strength involves no such rigorous tensing. The blow falls like a pliable cane with all one's bones at ease and muscles in a state of complete relaxation. Deriving from the muscles, the pathways of *ch'i,* tenacious strength is superior in every way to force.

PUSHING-HANDS PRACTICE: THE BASIC MOVEMENTS

The Pushing-Hands Practice (T'ui Shou) forms the basis of T'ai-chi as a sport. A match is played by two players, standing with feet fixed in place, facing each other. The object of the match is to uproot your opponent, causing both his feet to leave the ground, while remaining firmly rooted yourself. Although the match can be performed by players moving freely about, it is best for the beginner to commence study by learning several fixed and basic steps. The basic movements required in the Pushing-Hands Practice are the postures incorporated in Grasp Sparrow's Tail, namely Ward-off (to detect an opponent's moves), Press (to uproot an opponent), Rollback (to neutralize an opponent's attack), and Push (to uproot an attacking opponent).

Beginners usually find it difficult to distinguish tenacious energy from forceful energy. Pushing hands with a partner will bring appreciation of the distinction. Its basic principle is light adherence—no resistance and no letting go. In other words, light contact with the opponent's body is maintained without interruption. Each player is guided purely by his sense of touch. At your opponent's slightest pressure, yield to him; at his slightest retreat, stick to him. Your palms should be glued to him like a shadow to its object or an echo to its sound. Over a period of long and correct practice you will become able to anticipate his moves *before* he makes them.

The following photographs illustrate the Pushing-Hands Practice with fixed steps. For easy comprehension the players are termed A (Professor Cheng, in Chinese dress) and B (an associate). The photographs are reproduced in the conventional manner, not in the mirror images of Chapter IV.

Single-Hand Exercise

This movement is done by two players, each using one hand alternately. It is a preliminary exercise to the movements employing both hands which follow. A faces B at a distance of about three feet. B has his left foot advanced and his left arm in front of his chest, palm in. A steps forward with his left foot, raises his left forearm in front of his chest with the palm in, and attaches it lightly between B's left elbow and wrist. Both players rest their right hands beside their right thighs and concentrate most of their weight on their left legs *(Photo 127)*. B circles his arm clockwise (toward himself) and A follows; as it proceeds toward A, he yields, continuing the circle. Within this circular context the players may move their arms vertically and horizontally, their weight shifting from the front (left) to the rear (right) leg in the process. Remember, no force is to be exerted. Simply yield before and follow your opponent's arm without breaking contact. You use your waist and upper torso in the action, but your feet are fixed and do not move. Next, both players put their right legs in front and circle their right arms—this time in a counterclockwise direction. After a time, attempt to lightly graze your partner's shoulder with your circling hand. This should not be forced but done only as part of the circling. To avoid this touch, your partner will have to neutralize your effort with his waist.

127

MOVEMENT 2

Ward-off

Both players have their right legs forward. A raises his right forearm before his chest, palm in, and B's forearm adheres to it. The left hand of each player is held between the chest and right elbow, palm out. Weight is concentrated on the right legs. This posture is termed Right Ward-off *(Photo 128)*. It is not used to attack your opponent but rather as a feeler which, guided by your sense of touch, detects your opponent's move and enables you to defeat him by turning your waist and nullifying his attack.

128

129

MOVEMENT 3

Press

A is now on the right to better depict his hands.
When A uses Ward-off, B begins to attack. A then
attaches his left palm lightly to the middle of his
right forearm, shifts his entire weight to his right
foot, and with the momentum of his lower torso
presses forward against B's chest *(Photo 129)*. If B
neutralizes A's Press, A should stop, or he will be
unbalanced forward. If B uses strength or fails to
neutralize him, A uses Press to uproot him.

130

MOVEMENT 4

Rollback

If B neutralizes A's Press by turning left, circling the
arm clockwise, and beginning to push against A's
left forearm, A turns his waist to the right rear,
lowers his right elbow, and circles his right arm
counterclockwise until his right elbow touches B's
left elbow from the outside. The back of A's left
wrist adheres to B's left hand, palm in, and as B
pushes forward the palm is turned slightly up *(Photo
130)*. This, coupled with a slight overturning of his
right elbow and a withdrawal of the waist as the
weight shifts back to the left foot, permits A to neutralize B's push to the left rear. In his neutralizing
Rollback, A's left palm comes close to his chest but
does not touch it. The action of the arms, relaxed but
efficient, combined with a shifting of the weight to
the left foot, is indeed subtle. It is, so to speak, "cap-
turing the enemy after leading him into ambush."

MOVEMENT 5

Push

When A uses Rollback, B must stop his Push or be unbalanced forward. As he stops and begins to withdraw, A places his right palm on the back of B's wrist and his left palm on B's right elbow *(Photo 131)*. Looking directly forward, A pushes with the momentum transmitted from his lower torso and uproots B. If the Push is done incorrectly, it will be because: (1) A has not detected B's faulty move or has acted on it too late, (2) A has pushed without having a postural advantage and thus opposed strength with strength, or (3) A has neither detected B's defective move nor used his own postural advantage. Note that one of the four actions of Grasp Sparrow's Tail is always being employed throughout the exercise. If A uses Push or Press, B in yielding uses Rollback, and vice versa.

131

UPROOTING TECHNIQUE: Uprooting an oppo-
HOW TO PERFECT IT   nent so that both his
feet leave the ground requires a faultless technique. If only
his front foot is uprooted, causing it to wheel to the rear,
your technique needs improving. Carefully study the six
points presented below and apply them when doing the
Pushing-Hands Practice. In this way you should be able to
overcome any faults of technique.

1. Before attacking, you must withdraw slightly,
straighten your waist, and use tenacious energy. Your front
knee should not extend over the toes of your foot—otherwise your energy will be dispersed. With your shoulders and
elbows loose, keep your spine and your head erect. If these
things are done, your tenacious energy will be unified and
can break down any strong point of your opponent.

2. Don't use too much force when you touch your opponent before attacking. If you do, this will give him a chance
to anticipate your attack so that, as you begin it, he can neutralize your weight slightly and you will fail to uproot him.

3. When your hands lightly touch him, you must detect
a slight wave of resistance in his body. Taking advantage of
this wave, you will be able to attack him decisively. This

132

detection, however, is an ability requiring a long period of study and practice.

4. When attacking, don't use force with both hands. The *T'ai-chi Ch'uan Classics* say that in an attack it is necessary to aim at one direction of your opponent. To use force with both hands is technically known as "double weighting" and contradicts the principles of T'ai-chi. The correct way is to attack with one hand while the other simply touches the opponent's body lightly.

5. The position of your hands and arms relative to your body before attacking should remain the same after attacking. Any disproportionate stretching and contracting of the hands and arms will affect the unified action of the tenacious energy from your leg, and the efficacy of your uproot attack will be greatly decreased.

6. In attacking, you must first withdraw slightly to the rear and downward and then rise, pushing slightly upward, thus uprooting your opponent. The *Classics* says that if you want to push upward you must first go downward.

Photos 132–34 illustrate the techniques of the Pushing-Hands Practice as used to correctly uproot an opponent.

133

134

CHAPTER SIX

T'ai-chi for Self-Defense

Although the emphasis in this beginning text is on T'ai-chi as physical exercise, the student must not forget that T'ai-chi is closely related to the fighting tradition of Shao-lin Temple Boxing, and that every movement has its logic in a practical, combative use. Hence it is that the surest test of the efficacy of any of the many systems of T'ai-chi practiced today is simply to examine the postures from the standpoint of use: if they cannot be related to practical application, the system is clearly incorrect.

Because of its practical basis, the art is permeated with realism. Functional training may be gained through the Solo Exercise by imagining an opponent vying with you as you go through the postures. Your mind operates to create this imaginary opponent. If you disregard this vital aspect, your postures will lose meaning and *trueness,* and the exercise will become merely a mechanical charade.

Used imaginatively, the Pushing-Hands Practice, with its stress on interpreting strength, is highly effective training for self-defense. The postures used in it, however, are limited to four and these you have learned to use only in a sporting manner. How does T'ai-chi cope with striking, kicking, and grappling assaults done, not in sport, but in earnest? T'ai-chi's answer is that the principles underlying the Solo Exercise and the Pushing-Hands Practice, especially that of interpreting strength, have an equal, if not indeed a greater, validity in terms of self-defense.

INTERPRETING STRENGTH   The self-defensive application of T'ai-chi rests on your ability to interpret strength. It is difficult to explain the art of interpreting strength. The *T'ai-chi Ch'uan Classics* describe it in this manner: "At the opponent's slightest stir, I have already anticipated it." It is similar to the military tactic of "starting after the enemy but arriving before he does." When the opponent has committed himself to a move from which he cannot retreat, we detect it and attack before he does, thus thwarting his intended move and toppling him at the same time. There are six basic tactics to be distinguished in boxing: 1) the real or the false (the feint), 2) the solid (effective) or the hollow (mere parleys), 3) the big or the little, 4) the long or the short reach, 5) the rigid or the pliable, and 6) the use of inner strength or external force. These can be interpreted only after many years of gradual progress. Only the most proficient student is able to master the principle of interpreting strength to the point where only a single touch is sufficient to tell him all he needs to know about his opponent.

The proficient T'ai-chi student can arrive at the stage of what is technically called the application of "receiving energy." This is a complete negation of the notion of countering force with force. When someone throws a rubber ball at you, with a little force you can knock it away. Still, this is force against force. Suppose someone attacks you with an iron ball weighing five hundred pounds. Will force suffice to knock it away? The correct application of receiving energy is that when the iron ball comes near, you must first attract it like a magnet and then throw it away. The speed and the force you use must be very precise for the purpose. The interpreting, adhering, withdrawing, and attacking energies are all involved in an instant.

At an even higher level of interpretation, even the sense of touch is unnecessary. The master's body reaches such a state of perfection that it is able to dodge a blow by reflex action even if delivered from behind without warning. The reader—particularly the Westerner—may deride this as superhuman, but let us rather call it supernormal. It is within the reach of all, provided correct instruction and regular practice are employed. No special natural talent is necessary as a prerequisite. Orthodox boxing, in which speed and power defeat the slower and weaker, should not be mentioned in the same breath with T'ai-chi as an art of self-defense: the two are as different in method as night and day.

Care must be exercised, however, lest the method of application become an end in itself. The ultimate aim of T'ai-chi is to do without method—the response to an attack is a reflex done without cognition.

SELF-DEFENSE MOVEMENTS   T'ai-chi for self-defense can be best learned from a qualified teacher, particularly after one has mastered the Solo Exercise and the Pushing-Hands Practice. Therefore the movements illustrated on the following pages make no attempt at completeness, but these examples will serve to indicate the self-defensive use of some of the basic T'ai-chi postures.

In studying the photographs, again note that they are reproduced in the normal way, not in mirror images.

Step Forward, Deflect Downward, Parry, and Punch

B, with his right foot forward, strikes at A's chest with his right fist. A withdraws slightly and then takes a half step forward with his right foot. At the same time, with his right fist he deflects B's right fist downward, thus neutralizing B's striking force *(Photo 135)*. B lowers his right fist, circles it counterclockwise, and attempts to strike A's face *(136)*. With his left hand A parries B's right fist, steps forward with his left foot, and strikes B's chest with his right fist *(137)*.

135

136

137

138   139

MOVEMENT 2

Withdraw and Push

B pushes A's right arm with both hands. A puts his
left arm underneath his right arm, forming a cross
with both palms in *(Photo 138)*. A withdraws slightly
to neutralize B's pushing force *(139)*. A turns both
palms out, his right palm touching B's elbow and
his left palm touching B's forearm *(140)*. A pushes
forward with both hands while shifting his weight
forward to his right leg. The energy used must come
from the leg, not the hands *(141)*.

140   141

142   143

MOVEMENT 3

Squatting Single Whip & Golden Cock
Stands on One Leg, Right

B steps forward with his right foot and grasps A's left hand with his right. A withdraws, shifting his weight to his right foot. At the same time he withdraws his left hand to the front of his left thigh *(Photo 142)*. A stretches his left fingers toward B's groin. B withdraws to the rear *(143)*. A raises his body, grasps B's right wrist, and attacks with his knee *(144)*. A's right arm may be used in one of two ways: to deflect a left hand attack or to attack B's throat while trying to knee him. B takes his right foot to the rear to avoid A's knee. A then kicks at B's groin with his toes *(145)*.

144    **145**

MOVEMENT 4

Separate Right Foot

B steps forward with his right leg and strikes at A's head with his right fist. A grasps B's right hand with his right hand, pulls down, and kicks at B's right shin with his right toes. A's left arm is bent at the elbow, the fingers pointing upward to maintain balance *(Photo 146)*.

146

147

148

MOVEMENT 5

Fair Lady Works at Shuttles, Right

B steps forward with his right foot and strikes at A
with his right fist. A withdraws slightly and grasps
B's right wrist with his right hand from outside.
Simultaneously, A turns his left palm out and touches
B's right forearm *(Photo 147)*. A then takes his left
foot forward and at the same time pushes B's right
ribs with his right hand. A's left knee should be bent
so that tenacious energy can be developed from his
leg *(148)*.

149   150

MOVEMENT 6

Turn Body and Sweep Lotus with Leg

B steps forward with his right foot and strikes at A with his right hand. A shifts his weight to his left foot and begins to turn from left to right *(Photo 149)*. A grasps B's right wrist with his right hand, and his left hand touches B's right elbow. Simultaneously, A lifts his right leg and sweeps it clockwise at B's right waist. A's waist and thigh must be relaxed and sunk or the sweep will not be effective *(150)*.

CHAPTER SEVEN

Two Masters Look at T'ai-chi

YANG CHENG-FU'S TWELVE
IMPORTANT POINTS

1. Complete relaxation is all-important. In Chinese this principle is expressed by the term *sung*. The best translation of the term is "to relax," but even this definition is too stiff. You must relax your entire body. There should be no strength exerted anywhere except at a slight point on your scalp where you feel your head as though supported by an invisible string from above. If you can relax your sinews, the rest will follow in due course.

2. "To sink" *(chen)* is really the second step of *sung*. Originally the two were merged in one concept. To sink means to become more stable by emptying the strength from your upper torso into your legs. If you retain strength in your chest, your body will float and you can be toppled easily. It is not sufficient, however, to sink the strength. It is more important to sink the *ch'i,* an achievement which concentrates your mind and will enhance your every action.

3. The substantial and insubstantial must be differentiated. Double weighting must be avoided—keep your weight on only one foot at a time. If your weight is on your left foot, you must use your right hand in attacking and vice versa.

4. Your head and your spine must be straight. In order for the spirit of vitality to ascend to the top of your head, the head must be erect. Therefore, your head cannot turn or nod without the whole body moving. The spine likewise is a pathway of the spirit and is kept straight so that the *ch'i* and *i* (mind) meet at the top, making your body light and nimble. When you turn, keep your sacrum erect; otherwise, you will be unstable.

5. Your waist is the immovable center, the axis of all bodily movement. It must be kept erect but flexible.

6. The posture Grasp Sparrow's Tail is like two men sawing wood jointly. If one stops, the other must also stop. In the Pushing-Hands Practice, never resist. The sawing analogy has two meanings for this practice: (a) yield to your opponent, draw back, neutralize, and then follow him, inextricably attached; and (b) at his slightest move, anticipate and beat him to the punch. The latter, of course, can only come from the former.

7. Don't put your hands out aimlessly. Yang always said: "I'm not a shelf; don't put your dead meat on me." Relax, be light and nimble—then your hands will have meaning.

8. Follow the Daruma-Doll Principle. Relax, be boneless. If you are like a weighted doll, you cannot be pushed over. Your body is nimble and your foot rooted. Your center of gravity is sunk, and all energy is focused on the point of one sole. If you are not relaxed, however, you cannot root your foot.

9. Distinguish between tenacious energy and force. Tenacious energy comes from the sinews, force from the bones. Tenacious energy is soft, elastic, active; force is hard, inelastic, dead. When an archer shoots an arrow, the tension, not the arrow, is the important thing. That part of your body from your foot to your waist should be treated as one unit so as to concentrate your energy.

10. In the Solo Exercise keep your balance so that the ch'i can circulate better. The exercise must be done slowly and evenly, as though you were drawing silk from a cocoon. Rash strength and rapid movement will break the strand, just as they will break the exercise sequence.

11. In the Pushing-Hands Practice you must recognize and know the technique of your adversary. Differentiate the genuine attack from the feint. When you ward off, don't go too far out; when you roll back, don't let your opponent come in too close.

12. To defeat a thousand pounds with a trigger force of four ounces, you must use correct technique. If you pull the horns or ears of a thousand-pound cow, you will be unable to move it. However, if you attach a four-ounce string to its nose, you will be able to move the beast easily. If the cow is made of stone, however, even this will not avail. Correct technique will not work unless it is applied against a living creature.

QUESTIONS AND ANSWERS We sat and the master smiled. I had been told that he might answer questions if he was in the mood. "If you hit a bell with a pebble," he said, "you will get a small sound. If you hit it with a mallet you will achieve a large sound. Similarly, if you ask me big questions, you will get big answers." The onus squarely where it should be, I began.

STUDENT: In most fighting arts, students have invariably approached and surpassed the achievements of their teachers. Why is it that none of your pupils approach you? Indeed, irrespective of how rapidly some have progressed, all of them fall far below your level. What is the secret?

MASTER: You are right, there is a secret. But it is so simple as to be unbelievable. Its nature insists that you believe, that you have faith; otherwise you will fail. The secret is simply this: you must relax body and mind totally. You must be prepared to accept defeat repeatedly and for a long period; you must "invest in loss"—otherwise you will never succeed. I succeeded to my present state because I pushed pride aside and believed my master's words. I relaxed my body and stilled my mind so that only *ch'i,* flowing at the command of my mind, remained. Initially, this brought many bruises and defeats. In fact, in some matches I was pushed so hard that I lost consciousness. But I persisted. I followed my teacher by listening to and heeding my *ch'i.* In crushing defeat, I forgot anxiety, pride, ego. By emptying myself I gave the full field to *ch'i.* Gradually my technique improved. Then, and then only, did my responses sharpen so that neutralizing and countering were the work of a moment. My students either do not believe in this path or, if they do, they do not pursue it eagerly enough.

STUDENT: You make it all sound so easy. If the mind is "right" and the body relaxed, then progress must come, you say. But what of sheer hard work, regular practice, unremitting labor?

MASTER: To reach mastery one must have recourse to the things you mention; one must work hard and never leave off daily practice. But we must be careful lest we make the work of T'ai-chi synonymous with that of Shao-lin. The latter generally is muscle, power, and perspiration smothering the mind. T'ai-chi, however, asks that you work with its principles always in mind. It is not enough to allot an hour or two daily for practice; the practice itself must be done correctly. Otherwise, it is a total waste. My teacher, Yang Cheng-fu, had been taught by his illustrious father, Yang Chien-hou, and at age thirty was teaching a rich official in Shantung province. Here life was easy and Yang grew lazy and fat. During this dissipation he returned to Peking and reveled in a life of debauchery. His father heard of this and ordered him home, where he imprisoned Yang in a bare room, isolated from all and everyone. For four years he was kept there and permitted no visitors except his father, who came daily to practice the solo and joint-hands exercises, as well as the stick techniques of T'ai-chi, with the degenerate son. During this period his accomplishment was far greater than throughout his previous lifetime, and he came out of the room after four years able to defeat easily those senior students of his father who a few years earlier invariably beat him. He was now a great boxer and the greatness never left him, even though in later years he required little practice to maintain his efficiency. For this is a truism of T'ai-chi: if one progresses, there will come a point where mere physical practice is unnecessary. Reaching this point, one has breached the profound, and I will say no more on it now.

STUDENT: In doing the postures how does one know when he is relaxed?

MASTER: This is a subjective thing, this knowing, whereas the relaxation is objective. I would say a good start is made on relaxation when the student is able to go through a round without letting outside influences into his mind. But this is only the first step. The next step is to do the exercises in such a true manner that you are nearly exhausted at the conclusion. When your shoulders feel heavy you will know you are approaching real relaxation. This is a result of "swimming in air."

STUDENT: But do not the *Classics* say that the body must be so light that a feather will be felt? How do you equate this lightness with the exhaustion which comes from exercising against imagined resistance?

MASTER: There is no contradiction here although it does sound paradoxical. You could, of course, do postures for five minutes lightly and quickly and not be tired. This would not help you relax. By doing the postures slowly, correctly, and against an imagined resistance you tire, but in a real fight your body is freed of the resistance leash put on it by your mind and becomes incomparably light, sensitive, adroit, and quick.

STUDENT: As you know, I have learned T'ai-chi from several other teachers. I meant no disrespect to you, but since time was limited for both of us, and since I wanted to write of the varieties of T'ai-chi, I thought it wise to learn as much as I could. Most of these other methods employ auxiliary exercises to enhance correct breathing, the postures, and overall agility. Are such exercises beneficial?

MASTER: Only a teacher with a small art is jealous of a student's instruction elsewhere. I welcome your sampling of other systems, for I know you will come to realize that you really have but one master in this art. The postures themselves are so fully rounded, so variable, and so beneficial that additional exercises will only detract from your progress.

STUDENT: Is Shao-lin an excellent exercise and means of self-defense?

MASTER: If I thought so, I would do it rather than T'ai-chi. As exercise, its emphasis on brute strength and muscle strain impedes rather than builds health. In fighting, since it can never go beyond reliance on strength, force, and technique, it never achieves true superiority. Without egotism allow me to say that on the mainland in my younger days I frequently met the challenges of all manner of men and my art never left me.

STUDENT: Can one learn by watching?

MASTER: One can learn something but, of course, not all. Practice is necessary. In this respect, there is the story of Yang Chien-hou's neighbor, who secretly watched the T'ai-chi practice from his premises for several months and then asked one of Yang's students to attack him. When the student complied, he was ferociously pushed down by the neighbor. Yang saw it and asked where the man had learned the technique. His neighbor, amused, responded: "From you." A better story concerns Yang Lu-ch'an, perhaps the greatest of all T'ai-chi masters. Yang was employed by a druggist who had engaged famed T'ai-chi master Ch'en Chiang-hsiang to teach his sons. Yang secretly watched the practices and became so proficient that Ch'en accepted him as a full-fledged student.

STUDENT: How important is the Pushing-Hands Practice?

MASTER: Very important. You will not advance without it. But heed these things I tell you now about the practice. It is better to push with a child than with a technically skillful man who uses strength—which, of course, causes you to use strength also. In pushing with a child, regard him as a man; in pushing with a man, regard him as a child. This may sound paradoxical but it is not. The child affords you a relaxed partner to practice with, but, while benefiting from his "relaxability," you pretend he is like you, a man. This brings functional point to the exercise. Now, the other side of the coin. Why should one practicing with a man pretend he is a child? This is simply a diminishing process by which we rid ourselves of fear. It does not mean, however, that cockiness will succeed departed fear. We empty ourselves of fear and pride alike.

STUDENT: Isn't the Pushing-Hands Practice dangerous in that in it you permit your opponent to touch your body? In a real fight wouldn't this permissiveness be your undoing?

MASTER: No. The Pushing-Hands Practice is only a means to an end. It teaches tactile sensitivity and discrimination. But it also teaches distance appreciation. In a real fight you do not permit your enemy to touch you, but you work as close to him as possible so that you may counter easily. Some masters have what we call *receiving energy,* with which one's body not only absorbs an enemy's strike, but also repels him at the same time. Some higher masters have this ability under subconscious control, so that they can be attacked from the rear and the enemy repelled ten feet by the force of his own attack, with the master hardly being aware of it. This type of person has no difficulty in a real fight. The more ordinary player, though lacking this ability, will find that the Pushing-Hands Practice has sharpened his senses and that it permits him to fight close to his antagonist, but without permitting the enemy to touch him.

STUDENT: Chuang Tzu (399–295 B.C.) stated that a drunk

man escapes injury because his soul is intact. Isn't this protection what we seek in T'ai-chi? If Chuang Tzu is correct, wouldn't it be easier merely to become an alcoholic?

MASTER: To empty oneself is to conquer fear. This was one of the main goals of *wu wei*. This it was which enabled a Taoist, when he came to die, to build a funeral pyre and then calmly walk into the flames. (I interposed here that this quality of erasing fear was not unique to China. The lifelong discipline of the Japanese samurai was aimed at dying well, not to mention St. Lawrence, who, as he was being grilled alive, remarked to his torturers: "Turn me over, this side is done." The master acknowledged this with a smile and continued.) True enough, a drunk's inhibitions are released, his muscle tone depressed, and his body relaxed. But not entirely: a drunk will always find his way home. A drunk forfeits *i* (mind) and is thus at the mercy of circumstances. In T'ai-chi, on the other hand, we relax but keep an active *comprehending* mind.

STUDENT: Why didn't Yang Cheng-fu go to the West to make money with his skill?

MASTER: Once a Chinese doctor returned to Canton from the United States and implored Yang to return with him. Both, he said, could reap a huge fortune. Yang refused. The West held no allure for him, nor did money. He was so wrapped up in his environment he desired no change.

CHAPTER EIGHT

The T'ai-chi Ch'uan Classics

The *T'ai-chi Ch'uan Classics* comprise a rich but slim volume, numbering hardly more than a half-dozen pages. At least some parts of what follows are believed to have been written by Wang Tsung-yueh in his *T'ai-chi Ch'uan Lun* (Theory of T'ai-chi Boxing). The name of this book was later changed by the Yang family to *T'ai-chi Ch'uan Ching* (T'ai-chi Boxing Classics). The original document was found in a salt store in Wu-yang Hsien of Honan province by a brother of Wu Yu-hsiang in the last half of the nineteenth century. Wu, who had learned the old Ch'en Chia Kou style of T'ai-chi from Ch'en Ch'ang-hsing and Yang Lu-ch'an and the new style from Ch'en Ch'ing-p'ing, may have corrupted part of the text in acting as a transmitter of the new style.

Irrespective of what Wu may have done with the original, the *Classics* are our best link with the past of T'ai-chi. They are the basis of the art. By their very nature they are discursive and redundant but, at the same time, profound. In the present era, when T'ai-chi has proliferated into so many schools—many of which are unrecognizable from Shao-lin forms—the *Classics* can be used as a model. If these systems violate the *Classics,* the systems are wrong. Also, the reader will note that the *Classics* stress the function of the art. Currently, few books include any notion of the use of T'ai-chi as a fighting art. It is laudable to stress the exercise aspect, but not to the exclusion of practical use. Indeed, it may be argued that a man lacking the ability to use the art as a fighting tool can hardly be expected to be able to teach it as an exercise. The two aspects are too closely interwoven.

THE BODY AS ONE UNIT In any action the entire body should be light and agile and all of its parts connected like pearls on a thread.

The *ch'i* should be cultivated; the spirit of vitality should be retained internally and not exposed externally.

Sound boxing is rooted in the feet, develops in the legs, is directed by the waist, and functions through the fingers. The feet, legs, and waist must act as one. There should be no hollows and projections and no severance, so that when advancing and retreating you can use both your opponent's defects and your own superior position. If you fail to gain these advantages, your body will be disordered and confused. To correct this fault you must adjust your legs and waist. The same principle applies irrespective of direction or attitude.

T'ai-chi hinges entirely upon the player's consciousness *(i)* rather than upon his external muscular force *(li)*. When attacking above, you must not forget below; when striking left, you must pay attention to the right; and when advancing, you must have regard for retreating. This principle applies for both the attacker and the defender. If you want to pull something upward, you must first push downward, causing the root to be severed and the object to be immediately toppled. The substantial and the insubstantial must be clearly differentiated. Every part of the body has both a substantial and an insubstantial aspect at any given time. The entire body also has this feature if considered as one unit. All parts of the body must be threaded together, not allowing the slightest severance.

T'ai-chi Ch'uan is also called *Ch'ang Ch'uan* [Long Boxing] because it flows unceasingly like a great river. The eight postures of T'ai-chi* equate to the *Pa Kua* [Eight Trigrams] of the *I Ching*. Likewise, the first four postures represent the four directions: south, north, west, and east. The last four postures in turn reflect the four corners: southeast, northwest, southwest, and northeast. The five attitudes of T'ai-chi are Advance, Retreat, Look to the Left, Gaze to the Right, and Central Equilibrium, and equate to the five elements of Chinese philosophy: metal, wood, water, fire, and earth. Thus the eight postures plus the five attitudes are termed the T'ai-chi Thirteen Postures.

---

* The eight postures are Ward-off, Rollback, Press, Push, Pull, Split, Elbow, and Shoulder (see photos on the following page).

The Eight Postures of T'ai-chi
The first four postures or "directions" are the principal pos-
tures of T'ai-chi, as used in the Pushing-Hands Practice
(see page 80). The latter four are termed "actions" (see
preceding page) and, along with the former four, are studied
in detail in Ta Lu, a form of advanced practice which is
beyond the scope of this primer.

COORDINATING THE SUBSTAN-   T'ai-chi comes
TIAL AND INSUBSTANTIAL   from infinity;
from it spring yin and yang. In movement the two act independently; in stillness they fuse into one. There should be
no excess and no insufficiency.

You yield at your opponent's slightest pressure and adhere to him at his slightest retreat. To conquer the strong
by yielding is termed "withdraw" *(tsou)*. To improve your
position to the detriment of your opponent is called "adherence" *(chan)*. You respond quickly to fast action, slowly
to slow action. Although the changes are numerous, the principle remains the same. Diligent practice brings the skill of
"interpreting strength." Beyond this achievement lies the
ultimate goal: complete mastery of an opponent without
recourse to detecting his energy. This, however, requires
arduous practice.

The spirit of vitality reaches to the top of the head and
the *ch'i* sinks to the navel. The body is held erect without
leaning in any direction. Your opponent should not be able
to detect your change from substantial to insubstantial or
vice versa, because of your speed in effecting this change.
When your opponent brings pressure on your left side, that
side should be empty. The same holds for the right side.
When he pushes upward or downward against you, he feels
as if there is no end to the emptiness he encounters. When he
advances against you, he feels the distance incredibly long;
when he retreats, he feels it exasperatingly short.

The entire body is so light that a feather will be felt and
so pliable that a fly cannot alight on it without setting it in
motion. Your opponent cannot detect your moves but you
can anticipate his. If you can master all these techniques
you will become a peerless boxer.

In boxing there are myriad schools. Although they differ
in form and scale, they can never go beyond reliance on the
strong defeating the weak or the swift conquering the slow.
Yet these are the result of physical endowments and not
practical application and experience. The strong and the
quick, however, cannot explain and have no part in the de-
flection of a thousand-pound momentum with a trigger
force of four ounces or of an old man defeating a great number of men.

Stand like a balance and move actively like a cart wheel.
Keep your weight sunk on one side. If it is spread on two

feet you will be pushed over easily. Coordinating the substantial is the key here. If that is achieved, then you can interpret strength. After this, by practicing vigorously, studying, and remembering, one can reach the stage of total reliance on the mind. Forget yourself and yield to others. Go gradually, according to the right method. Above all, learn these techniques correctly; the slightest divergence will take you far off the path.

THE THIRTEEN POSTURES AND THE MIND The mind directs the *ch'i,* which sinks deeply and permeates the bones. The *ch'i* circulates freely, mobilizing the body so that it heeds the direction of the mind. If the *ch'i* is correctly cultivated, your spirit of vitality will rise and you will feel as if your head were suspended by a string from above, thus eschewing bodily slowness or clumsiness. The mind and the *ch'i* must be coordinated and blended with the exchange of substantial and insubstantial so as to develop an active tendency. In attacking, the energy should be sunk deeply, completely relaxed, and should aim in one direction. In standing, the body should be erect and relaxed, able to respond immediately to an attack from any direction.

The *ch'i* is to be directed throughout the body as if passing a thread easily without hindrance through a pearl having nine zigzag paths. The energy is mobilized like steel refined a hundred times over, enabling it to destroy any hard object. Appear like a hawk seizing a rabbit and with the spirit of a cat catching a rat.

In resting, be as still as a mountain; in moving, go like the current of a great river. Reserving or storing up energy is like drawing a bowstring; releasing it is like shooting an arrow. Seek the straight from the curved. The energy is accumulated before it is released and is developed from the spine. Action must be changed in accordance with the position of the body. To withdraw is also to attack. The energy is sometimes broken off but must immediately be joined again. Use the technique of "folding up"* when going forward or drawing backward. When advancing or retreating, turn your body and vary your steps.

* A hand technique in which, if an opponent pushes your wrist, you relax the wrist and attack with the elbow, or vice versa.

From the most pliable and yielding you will arrive at the most powerful and unyielding. Respiration must be correct so that your movements will be active and alert. The *ch'i* should be cultivated naturally and quietly. In attacking, the arms should be bent slightly and the energy reserved a little in order to prevent exhaustion. The mind is the commander; the *ch'i,* the flag; and the waist, the banner.

In practice, initially make big stretching movements and gradually reduce them to small compact movements. In this way eventually they will become perfectly fine and delicate. The old books say that if your opponent does not move, you should not move. At his slightest stir you have already anticipated it and are enabled to move first. The energy outwardly appears relaxed but is inwardly concentrated, ready to discharge at any movement. If the energy is broken off, the attention of your mind still remains. The mind leads and the body follows. The abdomen is relaxed, enabling the *ch'i* to permeate the bones. Your spirit and body are at ease, permitting you to heed the direction of your mind.

When you act, everything moves, and when you stand still, everything is tranquil. When you move, the *ch'i* adheres to the back of your body and gathers into your spine. Inwardly you concentrate your energy and outwardly you appear peaceful and quiet. Walk like a cat and mobilize your energy as if pulling silken threads from a cocoon.

If you absolutely ignore your breathing and pay attention only to your vital spirit, your striking force will be as strong as pure steel. If, however, you forget your spirit and heed only breathing, your *ch'i* will not circulate and your striking force will be greatly weakened. The *ch'i* is like a cart wheel and the waist like an axletree.

SONG OF THE THIR-   The thirteen postures should
TEEN POSTURES   never be neglected. Their
source is the waist. Change from substantial to insubstantial and back again carefully so the *ch'i* will flow without hindrance through your body.

When contacting forceful action you should move to meet it calmly. In this way you anticipate and counter your opponent's moves easily. Pay attention to your waist at all times. When the abdomen is completely relaxed, the *ch'i* can be directed outward instantaneously.

When the spine is held erect, the spirit of vitality reaches to the top of the head. Holding the head as if suspended by a string from above, the entire body feels light and nimble. If you carefully examine your postures, the movements of bend-stretch and open-close can be made automatically. Oral guidance by a competent master coupled with continual practice will bring you to a level in which skill takes care of itself.

What is meant by the correct method of body and function? The answer is that the mind commands and the body obeys. Remember well the chief purpose: the rejuvenation and prolongation of life. The above are the secrets of T'ai-chi; but pay heed lest you fail!

SONG OF THE PUSHING-HANDS PRACTICE

In Ward-off, Rollback, Press, and Push,
You must find the real technique—
If he goes up, you follow;
If he goes down, you follow—
Then he cannot attack.
Let him attack you with great force,
And use four ounces to deflect a thousand pounds,
Neutralizing him until he becomes powerless,
And then use withdraw-attack.
Also adhere and lift, support from below,
Stick horizontally, and attach from the rear—
Without letting go and with no resistance.

KEY TO THE FOOT-WEIGHTING DIAGRAMS

The foot-weighting diagrams that accompany the photographs of Chapter IV are designed to help you maintain correct balance of your body weight while performing the Solo Exercise. The key that follows explains the meaning of the eight weighting indications used.

Remember: in moving backward, touch the toe down first; in going forward, the heel. Then, as you shift your weight onto the entire foot, let the rest of the sole gradually touch the floor.

SEQUENCE DIAGRAM OF THE SOLO EXERCISE

This diagram gives an overall view of the directions you move in when performing the entire Solo Exercise. The numbers refer to the postures and the dots to the location of the advanced foot in each posture. Here you can easily see the directions in which you should move and learn to restrict your movements accordingly. Once you have learned the individual postures, the Sequence Diagram will remind you how to proceed in connecting the postures into the full sequence.

KEY TO THE FOOT-WEIGHTING DIAGRA

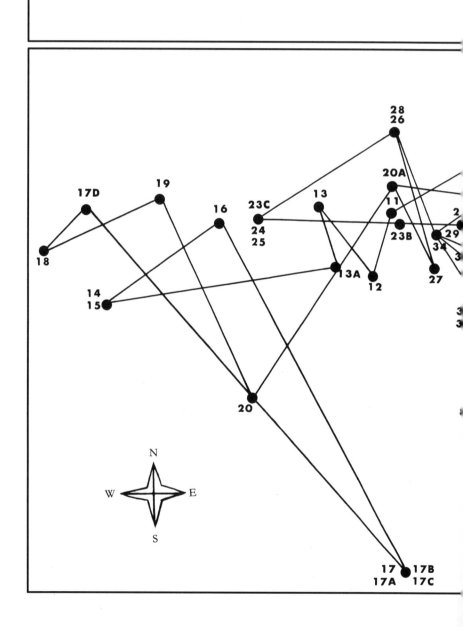

100%   70%   50%   30%

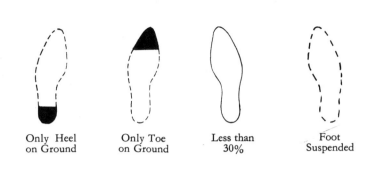

Only Heel
on Ground

Only Toe
on Ground

Less than
30%

Foot
Suspended

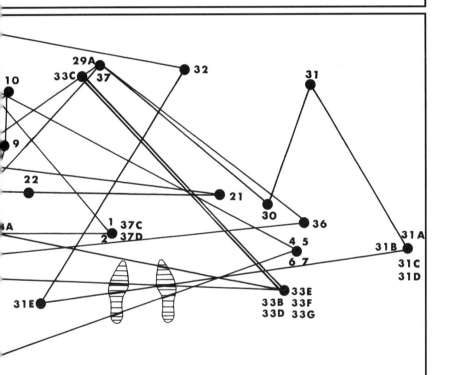

SEQUENCE
DIAGRAM OF
THE SOLO
EXERCISE

The *"weathermark"* identifies this book as having been planned & produced by John Weatherhill, Inc., 7 - 6 - 13, Roppongi, Minato-ku, Tokyo / Book design, typography & layout by John Dower & Ronald Bell / Composed by Kenkyusha / Platemaking & printing by Kinmei / Binding by Makoto / The type face used is Monotype Garamond, with display in hand-set Garamond

"Books to Span the East and West"

Tuttle Publishing was founded in 1832 in the small New England town of Rutland, Vermont [USA]. Our core values remain as strong today as they were then—to publish best-in-class books which bring people together one page at a time. In 1948, we established a publishing office in Japan—and Tuttle is now a leader in publishing English-language books about the arts, languages and cultures of Asia. The world has become a much smaller place today and Asia's economic and cultural influence has grown. Yet the need for meaningful dialogue and information about this diverse region has never been greater. Over the past seven decades, Tuttle has published thousands of books on subjects ranging from martial arts and paper crafts to language learning and literature—and our talented authors, illustrators, designers and photographers have won many prestigious awards. We welcome you to explore the wealth of information available on Asia at **www.tuttlepublishing.com**.